The Art of Competitive Pokémon

Table of Contents

Forward 5

Preface 9

Chapter 1: Your Journey Begins 17

Beginner

Chapter 2: Lower Beginner 31
    The Fundamentals 37
    Team Preview (Beginner) 49
    Leads (Beginner) 56
    The Dance 58
Chapter 3: Upper Beginner 71
    The Three Pillars 71
    Metagame (Upper Beginner) 85
    Expectations 89

Intermediate

Chapter 4: Lower Intermediate 95

    The Game Plan 96
    Purpose 100
    Team Preview (Intermediate) 102
Chapter 5: Upper Intermediate 133
    How to Practice Team Preview 133
    Leads (Intermediate) 139
    Automatic Information 147
    Double Switching 158
    How to Improve Your Battling 161

Advanced

Chapter 6: Lower Advanced 166
    Team Preview (Categorizing) 170
    Gathering Information 178
    Positioning 182
Chapter 7: Upper Advanced 187
    Deception 187
    Risk vs. Reward 192
    Strike 207
    Choke 209

Mastery

Chapter 8: The Master 213
    Patience 214
    Foresight (Extreme Awareness).....................218
    Never Rest on Your Laurels 221

Thank You 222

Foreword

Competitive *Pokémon* is, in a sense, a battle for information. The more information you can acquire about your opponent, the higher your chances of winning. In the same vein, the less information you reveal to your opponent, the better off you are. Indeed, the information that you possess can guide you not only in the teambuilding process, but also through the battle itself.

It then follows that, the ability to manage and process information quickly and accurately is one of the most important aspects of a *Pokémon* battle; which is why I believe this book will be useful for individuals who aspire to play *Pokémon* competitively.

Pokémon players of all levels can get something useful out of this book. I hope you enjoy reading it as much as I did.

- Gr8astard

Preface

Never did I think I'd be authoring a book, but I guess that's just a testament to the unpredictability of life. It has been one hell of a journey. Conjuring all the thoughts in my head and putting them to paper in a coherent and understandable manner was no easy task. Embarking on this endeavor has helped me grow a greater appreciation for those who produce creative work at a high level; If I had a hat, it'd be off to them.

The version of the book you're reading is my second attempt at this. Originally, I had written and published a different version, which I believed it to be solid. I put blood, sweat, and tears into writing it. Shortly after it was published, it was showered with praise. People were excited and appreciative for this new wealth of information. Fortunately for me, it wasn't void of criticism.

The most frequent criticism I'd receive was, "Solid read, but the book was a bit too broad and cliché. It didn't provide the kind of insights I was hoping for." I couldn't believe this. Rather, my pride wouldn't allow me to. I put everything a player needed to know in there, I know I did. Yet, for some reason, players were incapable of receiving the information in the way I intended. I brushed it off. I told myself, "They just don't get it". However, a part of me still felt hurt. I managed to bury this unease for a few months, but certain thoughts would keep reemerging whenever I'd think of my book. "Could I have done it better? Did I miss the mark?"

After all the work I put into this book, a "yes" to either of these questions would have left me in emotional ruin. So, I continued to avoid it. I couldn't face that possibility. It wasn't until I sat back and contemplated my original reason for writing the book that I was able to confront these thoughts. I had to face reality: the book wasn't that great.

My original purpose was to provide something that would allow any player to get to where they wanted to be. To up the game of the general player base. The issue was reality wasn't aligning with my original ambition. It was painful. I had to face that I had missed the mark. I was missing something crucial. Something I needed to connect with readers. I needed to understand the very people I'm trying to help. Only then could I reach them.

So, in embarking on the journey of re-doing the book, I became who I wanted to help. I, after about six months of not playing, retaught myself using the principles of the first book. It was rough. It was through that journey that this second book came to be.

It became very clear to me that there were a lot more details and nuances to this game of *Pokémon*. I, for the first time in years, was a sub-par player again. I struggled to do all the things that I would see my viewers struggle with. I made foolish mistake after foolish mistake. I lost repeatedly. Simply put, I sucked, and it hurt my pride. The fact that I could perform so badly after being one of the best to ever play this game was evidence that my skills were not due to inherent talent, but instead were the byproduct of the hard work I had put in. Through this process I discovered new techniques that can be applied to make the big ideological concepts more digestible, practical, and applicable.

I interviewed players of all levels of skill to find out what they struggle with the most and what they believe was stopping them. So much good has come from that failure.

Originally, I thought acknowledging that my first book was a failure would be embarrassing. However, due to that, it had allowed me to produce something that can truly change the game.

Throughout my years as a YouTuber, my main goal has been to imbed whatever knowledge of *Pokémon* I possessed into my viewers, hence my very detailed narration style. Many viewers even reported how much I have helped them improve. However, there has always been a block, I feel. I'd play the same loyal viewers and see them make nonsensical plays after nonsensical plays. It would baffle me. After repeatedly observing this pattern, the question then began arising: "Am I really making an impact?". This was a big deal for me. Impact was one of my core reasons for doing what I did. I needed it to be a "yes".

I then thought, "Perhaps there's a limit to how much a person can learn through viewing a video alone". That line of thought gave birth to the idea of a book. The hope is that this book will be the other piece to that puzzle. My viewers have done so much for me that it would require another book just to detail all that, so providing them with all the knowledge I possess was the very least I could do to show my gratitude and appreciation.

Some of you may be asking, "But Jam, why write a book?". Honestly, my true motivators for following through with this project were legacy and giving back. As a *Pokémon* YouTuber, I have a unique perspective when compared to most players and this perspective allows me to see players at many different stages of their development. As a result, I receive a wide array of questions. The goal of this book is to answer the big ones; to act as the *Pokémon* bible, if you will. My goal is to have the ultimate how-to manual with regards to *Pokémon*.

There is very little consistency amongst those who offer advice. One player will tell you to do *this*, while another will tell you to do *that*. Most people when attempting to give advice, tips, and tricks fail to fully contemplate the recipient's level of skill and experience. I wanted to direct people to core principles that exist. A place where there are only truths of the game; The Laws.

I often get questions on how to improve. I generally try my best to provide good answers, but I know, deep down, that they are insufficient in most cases. I always wished there was somewhere to direct people that could assist them no matter their level of skill and or experience. YouTube videos and *Pokémon* articles were options. Unfortunately, these would likely prove to be just as ineffective as my replies to comments. A book entailing all you need to know in chronological order is exactly what was needed. That way, no matter what phase a player was in on their journey, they could read and reference the exact material you need to get to the next level.

Chapter 1

Your Journey Begins

Before embarking on your journey to be the greatest *Pokémon* player the world has ever known, I'd like to impart some mindsets and philosophies that will be crucial to your development. Without understanding, applying, and accepting these truths, you will never achieve mastery.

Mindset

Firstly, you will need to adopt the mindset of a learner. This is key. Drop all ego at the beginning – no matter how experienced you are. When you adopt the mindset of a learner, also known as a "growth mindset", it will be just a matter of time and effort before you achieve mastery. The learner's mindset welcomes failures and views them as opportunities to improve; it welcomes the next hurdle because even if you trip and fall, you'll be better prepared the next time; it is open to the new and unfamiliar because in that discomfort lies progress. Potential is malleable. A loss is a learning opportunity for those who think like this.

Following that same line of thought, you will need to abandon the mindset of the finished product, also known as the "fixed mindset". If you ascribe to the fixed mindset, you will have a very difficult time experiencing improvement. This mindset believes ability is set in stone and rather than viewing failure as an opportunity to learn, one will shrink away from challenges and cast the blame onto things other than themselves. This mindset believes that failure means you are not good enough. In the case of a player that considers himself good, failure represents a threat to their identity. So, anything that could potentially lead to failure is avoided to protect their self-image. This mindset is poisonous and stunts growth. It believes potential to be fixed.

You may be thinking, "Why do I have to learn all this non-*Pokémon* related information? Isn't this a *Pokémon* book?" Yes, it is a *Pokémon* book. However, these mindsets are almost as important as the actual information. I learned all this from watching a presentation by Carol Dweck, the author of the book *Mindset*. Adopting the proper mindset will greatly increase how quickly you improve and the heights to which you ascend. Two players may start at the same time, both read the book, but one uses the non-*Pokémon* related and knowledge and one does not. The one that does likely experience a significantly faster growth rate. Here's an example to drive the point home.

Upon remastering *Pokémon*, I found that I would have a dull feeling of apprehension going into my battles. Weird, right? *Pokémon* is supposed to be this fun thing I do - a hobby, a leisurely activity, right? Then why would I be feeling this?

I later discovered that this feeling of apprehension stemmed to two things: my mindset and my reason. Prior to losing my skills, I had a fixed mindset. I believed myself to be the best. The negative aspects of my fixed mindset rarely manifested themselves because I won all the time but whenever I'd fall short, I'd chalk it up to something outside of myself make excuses. I'd tell myself whatever I needed to preserve my self-image.

Due to this, the process of regaining my skills was excruciatingly painful. Not because of any physical pain, but due to blows I would take to my ego. I would repeatedly lose to players who I perceived to be far below me; players of the past I would make quick work of. After so many losses, it became very apparent that I could no longer move forward with my current way of thinking. With the fixed mindset each battle became a potential threat to my self-image. My reasons for playing had changed, and I no longer viewed *Pokémon* as something fun. *Pokémon* was now something that defined a part of my self-worth. So, to stop the pain I had to do one of two things: Avoid playing or reframe how I viewed things. I had to change my mindset.

Moving forward, I began to view each loss as something positive. A loss now represented and an opportunity to learn, which was good! With this small tweak, I over time began to feel a decrease in feelings of apprehension and an increase in fun! Don't get it twisted, I still love winning and dislike losing. However, I wasn't operating with fear. I now chose to view a loss in an empowering light. As you, the reader, move forward I encourage you to do the same. It will be a far more enjoyable journey.

Journey

The second thing I'd like to emphasize is that this is a journey. You will not get there overnight. You will not get there by simply reading this book. After consuming the words, you don't then transform into a beast within a few minutes. It will require consistent effort.

You will not get there without consistency. There will be time investment. Try your best to enjoy every battle building up to your eventual mastery. You'll miss them. Trust me.

In the beginning you will suffer quite a few losses. Over time, you will start getting a few wins because you'll start to gain experience and learn the patterns. If you follow the principles in this book you will experience a big leap in your wins after a few weeks. This is where things get interesting. This is where what you're made of will be tested. At this point you'll be confident that you can become a Pokémon Master. After reaching a certain level, you'll go through a rough patch where you'll have a streak of losses and hardships. It'll feel as if you've regressed. This is what differentiates great players from the pack. You might then start to think about quitting. You will then start to doubt if it'll be possible. You will then believe you do not have what it takes. These thoughts are false. I'm telling you this from personal experience and from the experience of clients I have coached. It is imperative that you persist. After a little while, you will bounce back and go higher than you did prior to the drop. It's called a learning curve. This will happen all throughout your journey. Just know it's a part of the process. Persist.

Failure

Third, you will not get there without failing. You will need to be mentally prepared to dedicate hours of focus, failure, and review to internalize this information. This book will not replace effort. If are looking for a magic pill, then stop reading now. This isn't for you.

As I just mentioned, failure is a part of the process. I will not tell you not to be discouraged because you will be. That's a fact. It will begin to feel hopeless at points. You will start to have thoughts of, "Am I good enough?", "Is it worth it?", "Does this actually work?". These thoughts are natural and a part of the human condition. All I ask is that you don't give power to them.

If you follow what I teach and persist in the face of doubt, loses, and uncertainty, you will succeed. This is no different than people who want to lose weight and then quit after three weeks due not seeing the level of results they want. They failed the testing phase. They will now have lower self-confidence not only because they didn't lose the weight but also because they quit on themselves. Don't quit on yourself. You bought this book for a reason. Prove to yourself, for maybe the first time in your life, that you can follow through and complete something. Persist.

Seek Mastery

The final takeaway here is what it means to seeks mastery. To be the best you must win. To win you must beat all the Pokémon on the opposing team. This is obvious, but I still felt it needed to be stated. Your goal is not to see if a particular set will work, hope you do ok, or even have fun; your goal is to knock out every last *Pokémon* on your opponent's side of the field. You can use whatever method you like, but in the end, you must stand on top. That isn't to say all the aforementioned things can't also be desired, but they're not the primary concern of someone striving to be the best. It's called *battle*, and not *play*, for a reason. One may want to be the best and equally have fun, that's perfectly fine, but I do not believe one can place fun higher in priority and still hit the mark.

If your goal is not to be the best but to simply improve your general level of play, then that's ok; this book will help you just the same. I merely wanted to plant the correct mindset going forward for those who do seek greatness; for those who do love the thrill of battle and want to be the best they can be. It may seem silly, but if you're investing hours of your time into this, then isn't the decision to remain mediocre the sillier of the two? My most enjoyable moments in competitive *Pokémon* have stemmed from achieving victory, after a hard-fought battle where I had to push my mental faculties to their absolute limit. I had fun. I have yet to meet a person who has fun while continuously losing. Let's learn to win.

Now comes the *Pokémon*-related content. Crazy, right? This book will be divided into four different sections: Beginner, Intermediate, Advanced and Master. Each section focuses on a different level of skill and each level includes knowledge, skills, and insights that, if mastered, will elevate you to the next level.

Beginner

(Learning The Generalities)

Chapter 2

Lower Beginner

The Fundamentals

It is paramount that you have a firm grasp of the fundamentals. These will be critical to your success. Imagine, for second, a person whose goal is to build a house; they have their desired end goal but have no idea how to use any of the tools necessary for its completion. If they attempt to build the house at their current level of expertise, it will lead to failure. In *Pokémon*, similar rules apply. You will be unsuccessful as a competitive player, guaranteed, if this is not understood.

Here is another example: let's say you desire to get better at basketball, so you search up, "How to get good at basketball". You get several results on how to improve various individual skills, that if mastered, would eventually add up to you achieving your ultimate outcome which is: becoming a good basketball player. Cool.

Let's say you clicked a video on how to dribble around three players. This is great because one would assume a good basketball player would be able to do this, right? But, here's the issue: the video failed to tell you that you need to master basic dribbling skills along with five to six other skills before you're at the level to dribble through three players. The person giving the advice assumes you already have a mastery of the fundamentals. So, you end up following the advice, fail, and wonder why you're not achieving similar results.

You are not receiving similar results because your foundation is not as solid as the person trying to teach you.

When explaining, we tend to have our paradigm in mind. A person who isn't familiar with our worldview may struggle to understand it, even if the correct information is present. My mission with this book is provide a layout for your progression as a player. Much like being a good basketball player is made up a mastery of different individual skills, so is being a Pokémon Master.

The fundamentals are the informational parts of *Pokémon*. This includes knowing the types, knowing what they're super effective against, their weaknesses and their neutralities. Knowing the power, accuracy and after-effects of most moves; knowing every Pokémon's typing, weaknesses, movepool, and stats. It also includes knowing what each 'battle-usable' item does. Pokémon also can be cultivated and modified, so it is imperative that you understand how Efforts Values (E*versus*) and Individual Values (I*versus*) impact them. Each Pokémon, prior to battle, is your personal, customizable war machine. A Pokémon battle involves assembling a team of six or less Pokémon to take down your opponent's team. You're the commander.

Now, if you're completely new to battling, then what you just read will be overwhelming and seem complicated but fret not for these are not difficult to learn. I'm not going to go into detail on these topics in this book; this books focus is on mastering competitive play. If you lack this information, then I'd suggest you stop reading right now and go learn these things. All this information is easily attainable via informational

Pokémon websites such as *Serebii* and *Bulbapedia*, just to name a few. YouTube videos are also a useful resource that should be utilized.

It will not be necessary to use rote memorization to internalize the information word for word. All these things will come to you as you begin to play. This information will quickly become second nature with a bit of effort. These concepts can be grasped within the span of a few days, if not quicker. Simply, play a high number of games and repeatedly research what you don't understand. In the beginning, how good of a team you possess isn't what is important. How much you win or lose isn't important. You don't know anything yet, so this is expected. Losing a lot is part of the process. Naturally, you should use this time to gather information and enjoy yourself.

they are at basketball. This simply isn't true. It is a bit more complicated than just using height to equate to ability. In the same way, a Pokémon can have a higher base stat total than another but still be considered worse and/or used less. This is a hierarchy of efficiency, not power.

Within this hierarchy, there are tiers. Higher tiers will include the "best" Pokémon at the time – the most frequently used. Whereas, lower tiers will include the lesser ones – the least frequently used. It's akin to leagues in sports. There are lower leagues you can play in if you're not good enough to play with the best of the best. The only difference is lower tier Pokémon can be used in higher tiers, but the opposite is not true. The "best" Pokémon are banned from being used amongst the worst.

Over time, a culture begins to develop within the tiers. Each starts to function as its own domain, otherwise known as a 'metagame'. A Metagame is an environment that is produced as a result of interaction between Pokémon and the effects they have on each other.

In the real world, there are different cultures. Each culture has its own unique social norms. If a person immerses themselves in a culture for an extended period of time, they will begin to learn its ways and develop the ability to anticipate certain things because they occur frequently. They will begin to adapt in ways that allow them to cope or thrive in that environment.

A Metagame in *Pokémon* follows the same principles. They are *Pokémon* cultures. They are dynamic and always changing. A Pokémon's entire role can change depending on the Metagame it is being used in. This constant room for growth and change is one of the reasons I love this game.

Your Army

I know hitherto I was focusing a lot on a Pokémon's individual efficiency but let me make something very clear. One Pokémon will not be enough to win in most cases. *Pokémon* is a team effort. Each Pokémon represents a soldier and each solider has its own strengths and weaknesses. The soldiers will need teammates that foster their strengths and guard their weak points. The process of assembling soldiers into a unit that supports each other is known as "team building". It is at this point that they transition from six individuals to a team. I'll be using the word "army" to keep the military theme going.

The best part about all this is you're the general! You get to orchestrate all of this! When you have selected your six soldiers, you will then have your own personal army. With this army, you can then wage war against opposing armies with the aim of defeating them. This also means that your army will need to be able to survive in whatever metagame it is in. If you're fighting in an area that's snowing, it would be unwise of you to clothe your men in tank tops. If you're fighting in an area that is hot, it would be unwise of you to clothe your men in coats.

Environment matters. You will need to understand the conditions of your environment while assembling your army. They will need to have the necessary tools and strategies to weather the storm from opposing forces while dealing decisive blows. Hopefully now you understand why I went to such lengths to provide a detailed education on what a metagame is. With this context, you are now equipped to construct an army with the efficiency hierarchy in mind. If you blindly construct a team without considering its environment, then the likelihood of success drops significantly.

You can learn where each Pokémon stand on the efficiency hierarchy, in a metagame, by looking up a chart known as the "viability rankings". This is a chart constructed by a council of experienced players of a metagame that shows you how efficient each Pokémon - within that metagame - has the likelihood to be. Viability rankings are produced after a metagame has matured. Matured here means people have been playing said metagame for about three months and have developed a decent idea of what's effective. Mind you, these are just based on estimation, *not* hard facts. But it is useful tool, however, to provide you with a good starting point.

If a metagame is new, or new in comparison to other, then you may not be able to find viability rankings for it. The upside to this though, is that almost any Pokémon can be considered viable because the terrain is unexplored. It's like a season in sports. You can't make a proper ranking of the best teams until they've played a few games. The terrain may have changed or for whatever reason. Perhaps the team or player who was amazing last season may not be doing so well at present.

The best way to learn is to start! Learn through trial and error! Play! No amount of reading alone will make you a great 'teambuilder'. Team building is both an art and a science. You're trying to craft this beautiful image using six different images, but it also needs to be functional and effective.

Here is the simplified process. You will first construct your army. You will then go out into the "wilderness" to fight opposing armies. It is here that you discover the truth of your force's effectiveness. You may win some and then get battered in others. Through these experiences you begin to learn; through this process you will begin to edit your army with the aim of doing better the next time. After doing this repeatedly, you will notice patterns in the issues that you face. You will then revise your army in a way that solves these issues, so when you face the next army, you're better prepared. It is through the repetition of this process that you develop the ability to team build. After repeating this cycle over and over, you will eventually forge a force to be reckoned with. You will eventually forge a good team.

If team building isn't your thing, that is not a problem. There is absolutely nothing wrong with using someone else's team. The ability to build a team and the ability to play well are two separate skillsets. You can be good at one and subpar at the other. I will not go into extensive details on team building in this book, however the process I mentioned is a full-proof method on how to get started.

Now that we've gone over the knowledge component of the beginner level, allow me to arm you with some skills to help you transcend it.

Team Preview (Beginner)

So now that you've acquired the knowledge, let's start focusing on the more skill-based aspects. The dos and don'ts. I'm going to give you a basic run down of how to go about winning battles at the beginner level.

Let's say you have now gathered your army and are now facing an opponent. I'm going to assume that you already know your own army; that should be an obvious prerequisite, but if not, I'll tell you – know your army. What moves each Pokémon has, what items, what abilities, everything. Even if you are not the one who made it, it is critical that you look at each Pokémon and the army.

Question 1:

- **"Do I have Pokémon that have moves that are super effective against multiple Pokémon?"**

I'm going to cut the opponent's team in half for ease of explanation. Let us say at team preview, after looking at your opponent's team, he has a ground type, a water type and a grass type.

You ask yourself the question, "What Pokémon does a lot of damage to my opponent's team?" You look at the opponent's team again and ask, "Do I have Pokémon that have moves that are super effective against multiple Pokémon?"

Then you realize that the answer is a yes! You notice that you have a Pokémon that has a grass move –

which would be super effective against the opponent's water type and ground type Pokémon – and, that same Pokémon, has an ice move that is super effective against the grass type. That Pokémon would be considered as soldier that do a lot of damage to the opposing army. Now that you have awareness of that Pokémon, use it as often as you can do attack the opponent!

Question 2:

- **"Do I have a Pokémon with a type of move that the opponent has no resistances to?"**

Again, I'm going to cut the opponent's team in half for ease of explanation. Let us say at team preview, after looking at your opponent's team. He has a ground type, a water type and a grass type.

You ask yourself the question, "What Pokémon does a lot of damage to my opponent's team?" You look at the opponent's team again and ask, "Do I have Pokémon with a type of move that the opponent has no resistances to?"

You then realize that the answer is a 'yes'! You notice that you have a Pokémon that has a ghost type move. No Pokémon on the opposing team resist or is immune to ghost, therefore it is a soldier that the opposing army lacks a 'shield' for, in a way of looking at it.

Now that you've uncovered this, attack with that Pokémon! Do damage! Defeat your opponent before they can defeat you!

There are levels beyond these simplistic thought processes. But for now, this is where I want your focus. As the book progresses, I will introduce you to more advanced concepts. Each section is designed to build upon the last. This knowledge is foundational, but it isn't enough to erect the skyscraper called mastery; you will also need the foundational skills. Knowledge isn't power, it's potential power. You'll need to learn how to use that knowledge. This is where skills come into play.

Leads (Beginner)

Back to the battle. So, now you have the answer to the questions at team preview. The next step you'll need to take is to determine your lead. Generally, at this level, most players will choose their lead based on whatever their designated lead is, what they think their opponent will lead with, or to get up entry hazards. These are not necessarily bad in and of themselves and they have their time and place, though these methods generally don't consider how your team matches up with your opponent's. The point of the team preview is to help you determine what the best course of action will be.

At the beginner level your lead will only need to be a Pokémon that you believe does well versus the majority of the opponent's team. Much like with team preview, there are higher levels to this as with all the skills you'll learn in this chapter, but for now I'd like for you to concentrate on mastering the current level. I'm not going to spend too much time discussing the lead here. Choose your lead and get started.

The Dance

Ah yes, the dance. A battle involves a dance between the use of 'offensive' and 'defensive' tactics. Offensive tactics do not only refer to using actual attacks, but can also include status conditions, entry hazards and more. Defensive tactics refer to maneuvering your soldiers in such a way that you suffer as little damage as possible. Mastering this dance will require continual practice. Only through experience will the nuances begin to reveal themselves. It must be earned. Let's get into the steps.

Attack

The goal in a Pokémon battle is to defeat your opponent's army before they defeat yours, plain and simple. In order to defeat your opponent's forces, it is imperative that you damage them. This seems like common sense, however I wanted to make this fact extremely clear. This means, the moment you enter a Pokémon battle, your aim will be to do as much damage as possible. Knock them out one at a time; do this repeatedly until there is nothing left.

Hopefully now you see why it is necessary to determine what Pokémon are threatening to your opponent. Without knowing this, you will go into battle trying to find your way. If the general does not know where he is going, how can his army? The purpose of the team preview is to show you the terrain you are about to enter and your job as the general is to decide what actions you are going to take. So, when you have determined what soldiers are most lethal, deploy them.

In the ideal situation, you want to use moves that are super effective against the opposing Pokémon, however that might not always be an option. So, the next best thing is to use moves that are not resisted by the opposing Pokémon. Refer to the two questions at team preview.

You want to avoid using resisted moves on the Pokémon you are facing. Imagine a soldier using his finger to poke an opponent, while his opponent his retaliating with punches. Who do you think will win that bout? Remember, do as much damage as possible.

If this is a new concept to you, then stop here. I want you to focus on attacking for at least days. Go into battle and practice what you just learned. It's cool to read and understand, but that won't translate into battle unless it is done.

Each day do at least ten games. You can do more, but not less. That totals out to forty games in a week, minimum. It is very important that you do this. Life will happen at times and you won't be able to do your ten games for a day, so just add however many you missed to the next day. Don't make a habit of this, however. Doing ten games per day for four days a week is far better for your development than doing forty games once. Do it whether you feel like it or not. Establish that discipline. Just like anything, there's a process.

Pokémon, but at the beginner level the one you will be focusing on is 'switching'. If the opposing soldier has the advantage over your current one, switch him out. Yup, you can do that. You don't have to leave your Pokémon on the field once it is outside the Poké Ball. You can call it back and send out another. This is the primary skill used when defending in *Pokémon*.

Let's refer to the soldier example; if you have a soldier on the battlefield that is very good a fighting with his hands and deploy him, but the enemy deploys a soldier that uses a sword, then your soldier will be at a disadvantage. Do you leave him out there to just lose? No, you call him back and send out another soldier that is good with a sword or something better. It is the same in *Pokémon*.

Often, what you switch in will take very little damage from the opposing force. This is where the team building component comes into play. Your team should possess Pokémon that can switch into moves that other teammates are weak to.

Let's say your opponent has a fire type on the field while you have a grass type. You are now at a disadvantage. You can't do much damage – remember how important that is – and your opponent can do a lot of damage to you. It turns out you have a water type on your team as well. How can you solve this problem? How can you defend yourself against this fire type? You guessed right! Switch out your grass type into the water type! That way you take very little damage from fire attacks and you can now do a lot of damage with your water attacks! Problem solved.

Just like with the section attacking, do ten battles each day for four days. This time you're incorporating defending into it a bit more. This may not have been your first time switching, however now you're far more cognizant of it. You will home in on it more. The attacking portion will feel like second nature at this point, and so will defending. Remember to read the chapter before practicing every day.

This is the dance I was referring to. This is strategy! It's all about teamwork and you, the general, make the teamwork. It is your job to switch out soldiers that aren't in good positions; they are depending on you! Now you may be wondering, "What if the opponent switches out too? What then?" You know what, you get an A. Excellent question. And with that question, I will transition to the next topic.

Prediction (Beginner)

Ah, prediction. This is a fun one. Prediction is the final skill that you will be learning in your beginner training. Prediction is the act of anticipating what the opponent will do and then doing an action that counters that. Prediction is expectation. This is the money maker right here. With prediction, the game of *Pokémon* becomes a lot less linear and a lot more dynamic. So, instead of knowing exactly what your opponent will do and just falling into their trap, you can now thwart their plan.

To know when to predict you'll need a good deal of experience playing. You'll need to experience what people generally do whenever they come across certain Pokémon. It is through the learning of these patterns that you'll develop the foresight to know what exactly you're about to counter. It's putting yourself in the head of the opponent. It's asking, "If I were my opponent what would I do?" That question summarizes all that prediction is about. You predict when you want to disrupt what you believe your opponent will do. You predict when you want to gain an edge or a further advantage.

Let's say you have a water type on the field and your opponent has a fire type. Your water type has an ice type move. If whenever you have your water type on the field, people tend to switch into their grass type, you can then begin counter that by using your ice type move. Instead of using the water move to damage the fire type on the field, you anticipate your opponent to switch into his grass type and use an ice type move. This way you deal super effective damage on something that was supposed to counter you! So now you have the upper hand! This is why prediction such a beautiful thing. With this skill, ironically, the game becomes less predictable.

For prediction, still do ten games per day, but only for three days. So, thirty games in all. This is a skill that I don't want you to get consumed with because it can create bad habits. I just want you understand it.

After those three days of prediction practice, play for another four days. In this session, you won't have to focus on any particular skill. Your aim is simply to win as often as you can. If you find yourself struggling to perform the skills, then revisit the section you are struggling with the most. If you feel comfortable performing them, then great! You've graduated from the low beginner level! Proceed forward.

Chapter 3

Upper Beginner

The Three Pillars

In *Pokémon*, there are three pillars that are critical to the development of any player. These are 'knowledge', 'awareness' and 'skill'. I discovered these after pondering on what causes some players within the same 'tier' to perform well more consistently than others. Why can a player who's been playing for years be far worse than one who has only been doing it for months? I've discovered that the difference between players comes down to their level proficiency in these three categories.

Knowledge

The pillar of knowledge is predicated on actual information. It is knowing what exists, the types, the weaknesses, a move's power, how much damage a Pokémon may take from certain moves, everything. That obviously was not an exhaustive list; its goal was merely provide examples. In *Pokémon*, there will always be more things to learn. You may reach a cap with regards to the knowledge that the developers placed in the game, but with regards to the metagames and their evolution, staying up to date is a must. The more you know, the better.

Now, this isn't to say that you need to know everything to win or be great, but it does mean the more you do know the greater the likelihood of you succeeding. I sometimes refer to knowledge as the most vital pillar because it is the most foundational. Knowledge holds power in the case of *Pokémon*. This will make sense as you learn about the others, but for now just soak up this information. Studying and exposure is the best way to improve knowledge. You can do this by reading up on whatever it is that you want to know or learn it second hand by watching another player talk about it. These are two ways amongst many that it can be acquired.

Skill

The second pillar of skill is predicated on the what to do and when to do it. Ultimately, there aren't very many skills in *Pokémon*; it's how and when they are used that determine their effectiveness. Skill in this context is the ability to get the opponent to do what you want or to execute on your own game plan. Meaning, can you get your desired result?

Where knowledge is the information you know, skill is the action you take. What are you going to do to get the outcome you want? And as I mentioned earlier the merit of your actions are determined by when they're performed. Two people can perform the same skill but do them at different times and yield different results.

It's like in boxing or any combat sport. Often, it isn't the surprise factor of a new skill that does an opponent in, but a familiar move performed at the appropriate time. Effectiveness is the measurement of a skill. Was it effective or not? Effectiveness is defined by whether that action produced the desired result. Someone may perform a skill, but it backfires and leaves them in a worse position.

This is where the timing component comes into play. Let's use the skills of switching and predicting for example. These are necessary to be great at this game, however it goes beyond the question of, "Will I need to use the skill of switching or predicting?". The question then evolves into, "When do I switch and when do you predict?" You can predict and switch all day, but if it isn't aiding you in your victory then the timing needs to be reassessed.

Developing this will ultimately come down to experience. Because of the multitude of scenarios and variables in each game, it is difficult for me to instruct you on the precise moments you'll need to use a particular skill. There are a few ways to assess whether a switch or a prediction will be worth it however, and those will be discussed later in the book. I will also admit that despite all the theory and processes that are presented, there is an element of "following your gut" or 'instinct' in *Pokémon*. Ideally, you want to minimize relying on it, but I cannot deny its existence.

Going back to the boxing example, after continual fighting eventually you'll develop an instinctual understanding of what you feel an opponent will or won't do – key word here being feel. There is no conscious, rational explanation. Generally, you want to approach games in a rational manner with a concrete plan of execution taking as little risk as possible.

The skill pillar's timing component will only be developed by playing. There is no shortcut to this one. You can watch other players and learn secondhand to a certain degree, and this is encouraged, though that will only go so far. You must get in the ring and discover the nuances for yourself.

Awareness

This third pillar is probably the most interesting and unexpected of the bunch. Upon thinking about what distinguishes players, skill and knowledge just didn't quite cover everything. Players will possess a high degree of skill and knowledge, yet struggle with applying them in the appropriate situations, thus causing all that knowledge and skill to be ineffective and damn near meaningless. I can't recall how it came to be, but it was during that process that I discovered the third pillar, being awareness.

Awareness relies on realizing that there is something to be done. One may possess the knowledge and the skill to act on something, but if one is unaware of the opportunity to utilize these then it's useless. It seems to simple, but it's not until you're in battle that you will realize how detrimental this is.

Have you ever had a battle where you allowed a Pokémon to faint or take serious damage that it wasn't supposed to? What happened? Did you lack the knowledge? No. Otherwise, you wouldn't have known that it wasn't supposed to take damage. Did you lack the skill? No. You knew that you only needed to switch to prevent that. So, what happened? You lacked the awareness. You didn't realize or remember that you were supposed to prevent that damage. In that moment, you didn't realize there were alternative options. This is a massive game changer. This can be the difference between a player being intermediate and a master. It's that important! Awareness calls upon knowledge and skill. Awareness dictates results!

Let's use the example of a chariot. Knowledge is the chariot, skill is the horse, and awareness is the charioteer. The horse can guide the chariot, but it has no proper direction without the charioteer. If you have the knowledge of what to do and the skill to make it happen but are unsure of appropriate time to deploy the skills, then your results will be inconsistent.

In order to improve awareness, one needs to ask questions. The question you ask will depend on what you want to become aware of. We discussed this earlier in the book when you were learning team preview. Remember asking, "Do you have Pokémon that have moves that are super effective against multiple Pokémon?" That's bringing awareness to that aspect of the game.

How high your awareness gets depends on how high your skill and knowledge get. They are all interconnected. The more information you know, the more you're capable of being aware of; you can't be aware of something you don't know exists. Similarly, as your skill improves, your awareness improves as you will begin to notice the proper timing for actions to be taken. Remember, these are not mutually exclusive.

In this concept's earlier stages of development, I consulted other reputable players to see if there was anything I was missing. One player asked if experience could be another potential pillar. After serious thought and consideration, I concluded that experience is not a pillar, however it is the catalyst and the fuel for all of them. Experience is necessary to develop knowledge, with regards to actual play, and knowledge births skill and awareness. Experience is also what will be necessary to improve proficiency in all the pillars. This is not to say that experience is all that is necessary because it is not; you will still need deliberate practice.

With these three pillars, you can perform a self-assessment of not only where you are, but also what you did incorrectly. If you discover an error in how you executed a game, you can trail that error back to a lapse in one of these pillars. You either didn't know what to do or didn't realize that it needed to be done. Knowing this alone places you a cut above the rest!

Upper Beginner: Metagame

Now that you are familiar with the three pillars, let's tie it back to previous topics to help improve your understanding. Earlier in the book we discussed metagames, what they are, how they develop, etc. I did not introduce the pillars at the beginning because I felt a complete beginner may need some context and experience before it would make sense. Here are how the three pillars tie into the metagame discussion.

It is important to note that metagames are very knowledge heavy. This is the most important pillar when entering a new environment. If you do not have the knowledge of what to expect within that 'culture', then you will not know the appropriate actions to take; you won't know when to use your skill. Every to what degree they are common is invaluable. Every three months something known as 'usage statistics' are released for each tier. This is simply a document that shows you how often all the Pokémon have been used in that tier. It can be found on the Smogon website, or by Googling. Another useful learning tool is playing and/or consulting experienced players of that metagame.

The Pillars: Expectations

So now you have all this newfound insight and you're pumped! With great information comes great responsibility! Now that you logically understand it, you will now break free and become the master you always knew you could be, right? Probably not. There will be learning curve. During this phase of your journey I'm going to tell you what to expect. This section exists to provide you with a dose of reality. If you know what to expect, the likelihood of you giving up during hard times decreases. You won't take the failures personally, but instead know that it is par for the course

In your upcoming battles, you may begin to assess your decisions based on the pillars. Due to this new information you may find that the speed at which you battle has slowed down. This is due to the new processing taking place in your brain. You may not have realized it, but prior to this a lot of the actions and thoughts you had during a battle were what I call "auto-piloted" thoughts. This means these thoughts came to your brain quickly based on previous experiences. Now that you're disrupting these auto-piloted thoughts, the decisions you make are more intentional, thus leading to a slower processing speed.

Another side effect to this may be a small to significant drop in your average rating. Fret not and keep persisting. This is the trap most players tend to fall into when implementing something new. They stop doing that thing and make the claim that it does not work. The reality of that situation is that they simply didn't become proficient at it. This will then lead to them going back to their old habits and remaining where they were. There is no "one thing" or "magic pill". Just remain consistent with the laws of this book and you will succeed. These are not theories. I have tested them on my clients and instructed them on the what to do and they saw tremendous results by following the process. If you experience a dip in your rating, don't be alarmed. It's a part of the process. As you begin to master the application of the principles, you will far exceed what your previous plateau was.

I decided to put this in because you're still a grasshopper and I don't want you to become discouraged. I want to let you know that if you don't get it right away that it's normal. You're not a useless tub of lard. Or maybe you are, but not at *Pokémon* at least. This is very learnable. You can expect to meet failure as you begin to integrate this new information into your play. You may not see a rapid increase in your wins immediately, in fact they may decrease for moment, but so long as you get back in the ring and continue trusting the process I've laid out, you will get it.

It's like anything in life. Remember when you first tried to walk? Probably not, but let me assure you, you sucked. You sucked so much you moved around on your knees, but what happened? Did you quit? No. I would say don't be a baby, but a baby might be more mentally tough than you. Don't be a big baby. Step up and earn this. I'm not asking you to do anything I didn't do or any of the other thousands of players didn't do. I believe in you.

After pushing through and doing the repetitions you will notice crazy insights. That's how things work.

When you were a baby you crawled until the faithful day when you walked. Simple stuff, really. Nothing new. Execute and don't make excuses.

Intermediate

(Learning to Be More Purposeful)

Chapter 4

Lower Intermediate

Welcome to purgatory! Kidding, kidding. Welcome to the intermediate section of the book. You're now a player that has a firm grasp of the basics and now seek the skills to go beyond that. As the book proceeds, each subsequent chapter will have a lot less introductions. The earlier chapters required a lot of clarity, but now I trust that your foundation is sound. Let's proceed.

The Game Plan

"The art of war teaches us to rely not on the likelihood of the enemy's not coming, but on our own readiness to receive him; not on the chance of his not attacking, but rather on the fact that we have made our position unassailable." - Sun Tzu

The 'game plan' is the road map that will guide all your actions. A game plan is simply the actions you intend to take to defeat your opponent. This should be present in your mind before you choose your lead. I excluded this in the earlier chapters because you were just beginning. At this point you should be comfortable with the metagame you've chosen; now, you will begin to use the information and experience you've acquired to make plans.

If someone were to ask you for directions, you'd only be able to tell them where to go if you've explored the terrain yourself. In *Pokémon* it's very similar; the more experience you have the better. This isn't to say in order to win a battle you'll have to have been in that exact situation before, it just means you'll be able to better come up with solutions. It doesn't have to be super intricate, though the more intricate the better. It is meant to be the road map to guide your actions.

Going back to the pillars; the more knowledge and awareness you possess, the greater your chances of winning. During the game you'll be guided by your game plan. Each action will be taken with the plan in consideration and with the aim of achieving that goal.

Purpose

"There is a proper season for making attacks with fire, and special days for starting a conflagration." - Sun Tzu

What's the *why* behind your plays? 'Purpose' is the reason for which something is done or created or for which something exists. In the beginner section we focused a lot on just gaining the experience; in the intermediate section we will be focusing on being more deliberate with your actions.

Pokémon is a game of strategy. At its core, successful competitive battling is comprised of developing teams, formulating game plans, and executing. Of course, there are more facets, but fundamentally that's all it is. You want to take actions that aid in the progression of your game plan.

Purpose can be applied to just about anything that you bring into battle. This could include but is not limited to Pokémon, items, abilities, etc. How each of these things are used will be determined by the game plan that has been formulated. I will explain how these play into the battle a little later, but I wanted to get you acquainted with the idea here. This also goes hand in hand with the next concept that you need to understand.

Team Preview (Intermediate)

The team preview is the great decider. Prior to battling an opponent, you will be able to briefly view which Pokémon they have decided to put on their team. This is the true beginning of the battle, not when the first Pokémon enters the field. Remember that. We had a brief overview of the team preview in the beginner section and now it's time to take it to another level.

During the team preview, you have the opportunity to devise a plan for victory. This is imperative. With a game plan, each action will have purpose. Each move you make will be done with the intention of achieving whatever outcome you set. There is absolutely no downside to planning beforehand. The likelihood of emerging victorious can only increase. To not have a plan is to voluntarily place yourself at a disadvantage.

In the book *The Art of War*, an ancient treatise on combat, author Sun Tzu makes the assertion that, "The general who wins the battle makes many calculations in his temple before the battle is fought. The general who loses makes but few calculations beforehand". This isn't to say that you cannot be flexible throughout a battle but having a general idea of the outcome you want is always helpful.

There are benefits to having a game plan extend far beyond solely defeating your opponent. It also aids in protecting yourself against defeat. By sizing up your opponent in the beginning, you're able to approach the game with a heightened sense of awareness; you've considered, beforehand, where your weak points lie.

Going into a fight with a good sword and no armor is not supreme excellence. Now, let's get into the nitty gritty of the 'how to'.

The Two Questions

After absorbing the opponent's team, there are two questions you want to ask yourself: "What can't he guard against?" and "What can't I guard against?". These two questions are meant to be a tool to help create your road map as you enter battle. Assuming you have knowledge of that metagame, these questions will always bring important information to the forefront of your mind. Think back to the pillars. By asking yourself these questions, you're withdrawing, from your pool of knowledge, the answer to these questions.

After this, you bring the answers from your knowledge into conscious awareness. Now that they're in your awareness, you can employ the necessary skills to get the job done. Thus, the interaction between the pillars. Deficiency in one will handicap you in battle.

Always refer to these questions at team preview.

What Can't He Guard Against?

"You can be sure of succeeding in your attacks if you only attack places which are undefended" – Sun Tzu

Both questions focus on offensive capabilities: your offensive capabilities and your opponent's offensive capabilities. In *Pokémon*, offense wins championships. This is not to disregard the value of good defenses. Defense is also very important; however, you can't beat an opponent you never attack. In this section we will be focusing on the question, "What can't he guard against?" first. While sizing up your opponent's team, you want to look out for one of these four scenarios:

Scenario 1:

- "Do I possess a Pokémon that guarantees me a kill every time I choose to attack?"

Scenario 2:

- "Do I possess a Pokémon that 2HKOs (Knocks out in the two hits) most or all Pokémon on the opposing team?"

Scenario 3:

- "Do I possess a Pokémon that guarantees me victory if certain Pokémon are weakened to the point where they can no longer act as a reliable means of protection?"

Scenario 4:

- "Do I possess a Pokémon that guarantees or greatly heightens my chances of victory, if a particular Pokémon is completely removed by means of a partner Pokémon?"

Scenario 2

- **"Do I possess a Pokémon that 2HKOs (Knocks out in the two hits) most or all Pokémon on the opposing team?"**

At team preview you notice that your opponent possesses a team of three Pelipper and three Clefable. You have a team of five Ditto and a Tapu Koko. The Tapu Koko is equipped with the item Choice Specs. The Ditto are irrelevant to the scenario and were merely selected as fillers. All Clefable have the item Leftovers. All the Pelipper have been confirmed to possess the item Leftovers, so no matter what, Tapu Koko will OHKO with Thunderbolt due to it being four times weak to electric moves.

Looking at the team preview you ask the question, "What can't my opponent guard against?". In a situation like this, the opponent cannot guard against Tapu Koko. It can OHKO all the Pelipper and it can 2HKO all the Clefable. Knowing this, your game plan will be to get Tapu Koko in safely and use Thunderbolt.

You lead with Tapu Koko while your opponent leads with Pelipper. Turn one: the opponent switches out Pelipper into Clefable. Tapu Koko used Thunderbolt and Clefable Takes 85%. Turn Two: Tapu Koko uses Thunderbolt. Clefable Faints.

That's it. The opponent's Clefable may be able to take one hit from Tapu Koko, however that doesn't mean it can guard against Tapu Koko. When Tapu Koko comes in it guaranteed an OHKO or 2HKO on something. Therefore, during team preview it should be highly valued.

Scenario 3

- **"Do I possess a Pokémon that guarantees me victory if certain Pokémon are weakened to the point where they can no longer act as a reliable means of protection?"**

At team preview you notice that your opponent possesses a team of four Pelipper one Gliscor, and one Mew. Gliscor is equipped with the item Toxic Orb. Mew is equipped with the item Leftovers. You have a team of four Ditto, one Landorus-Therian, and one Tapu Koko. Your Landorus is equipped with the item Leftovers. Tapu Koko is equipped with the item Life Orb. All the Pelipper have been confirmed to possess the item Leftovers, so, no matter what, Tapu Koko will OHKO with Thunderbolt due to Pelipper being four times weak against electric moves. The Ditto are irrelevant to the scenario and were merely selected as placeholders. Tapu Koko can OHKO every Pokémon on the opponent's team, but for this to happen Mew needs to have 60% or less of its health and Gliscor needs to have 80% or less of its health. Tapu Koko's Thunderbolt and Hidden Power Ice KO both Pokémon from those percentages.

Looking at the team preview you ask the question, "What can't my opponent guard against?". In a situation like this, the opponent cannot guard against Tapu Koko. It can One Hit KO every Pokémon on the opponent's team assuming Mew is weakened to at least 60% and assuming Gliscor is at 80%. Knowing this, your game plan will be to weaken those Pokémon so that Tapu Koko can defeat the opponent with the combination of Thunderbolt and Hidden Power Ice.

You lead with Landorus-Therian while your opponent leads with Gliscor. Turn one: your Landorus uses Hidden Power Ice which brings Gliscor to 48%, while Gliscor goes for Knock Off doing 10%. Landorus lost its Leftovers. Turn two: the opponent switches out Gliscor into Mew to prevent it from getting KO'd by another Hidden Power Ice. You anticipate this and use the move U-Turn instead which deals 50% of damage to Mew. You then send out Tapu Koko. Mew restores 6% of its health from Leftovers leaving it at 56%.

Now, remember the conditions that needed to be met? Mew needed to be at 60% or lower to be KO'd by Tapu Koko's Thunderbolt. Gliscor needed to be at 80% or lower to be KO'd by Tapu Koko's Hidden Power

Ice. Now that all these conditions have been successfully achieved. Tapu Koko can now proceed to OHKO every Pokémon on the opponent's team. This focuses on using other members of your team to damage specific Pokémon which will allow another Pokémon to become more lethal. I must reiterate that these examples are very simplified. The goal was to make the concept clear. Through practice, and only through practice, will the ability to do this in more complicated situation develop.

Scenario 4

- **"Do I possess a Pokémon that guarantees or greatly heightens my chances of victory, if a particular Pokémon is completely removed by means of a partner Pokémon?"**

At team preview you notice that your opponent possesses a team of five Pelipper and one Electivire. The Electivire is equipped with the Item Life Orb. You have a team of four Ditto, one Dugtrio, and one Tapu Koko. The Dugtrio is equipped with the item Focus Sash. The Tapu Koko is equipped with the item Choice Specs. The Ditto are irrelevant to the scenario and were merely selected as placeholders. All the Pelipper have been confirmed to possess the item Leftovers, so, no matter what, Tapu Koko will OHKO with Thunderbolt due to Pelipper being four times weak against electric moves. Tapu Koko has three electric moves and U-Turn. Dugtrio has Earthquake. Earthquake OHKOs Electivire. Five of the opponent's six Pokémon cannot guard against Tapu Koko, however the Electivire, who possess the ability Motor Drive, is immune to Tapu Koko's electric moves.

Looking at the team preview you ask the question, "What can't my opponent guard against?". In a situation like this, the opponent cannot guard against Tapu Koko. It can OHKO every Pokémon on the opponent's team if Electivire is removed. Knowing this, your game plan will be to use Dugtrio to remove Electivire, then have Tapu Koko use Thunderbolt.

You lead with Tapu Koko while your opponent leads with Pelipper. Turn one: your opponent switches his Pelipper out into Electivire anticipating the electric move, but instead Tapu Koko uses U-Turn as you switch in your Dugtrio on Electivire. Turn two: Due to Dugtrio's Arena Trap ability, Electivire cannot switch out and proceeds to get OHKO by Earthquake. Now Tapu Koko can freely click Thunderbolt and guarantee a kill with no resistance.

That's it. This scenario focuses on the removal of a Pokémon, so that another Pokémon on your team can thrive. It will not be this simple in most cases, but it is important that you have a firm grasp of the concept.

The "What can't he guard against?" question focuses on leveraging the offensive power you possess and unleashing it on your opponent. It's an overwhelming force. Being an overwhelming force means you can muscle through your opponent's defense. You can knock out all six of your opponent's Pokémon before they get the opportunity to knock out all six of yours. You may not have checks or counters to their Pokémon, but your overabundance of power supersedes that. Your primary focus using this method is to not necessarily be defenseless, but instead be more destructive.

An example of this would be a person who, during a fist fight, lashes out with a flurry punches with little to no regard of how much damage they're taking. Their primary focus is to knock the other person out with powerful punches before they succumb. They deliver blows that are effective not because the opponent is weakened, but because their defense is not as strong as their offense. In the end, they are victorious. Teams that focus on using this as their primary method of winning are known as 'offensive teams'.

There are team types that employ a combination of both these methods to varying degrees. These are known as 'balance teams. I will not go into teams in this book, but I do think that bit of information was worth mentioning.

What Can't I Guard Against?

"You can ensure the safety of your defense if you only hold positions that cannot be attacked" – Sun Tzu

Ok, now let's focus on the defensive end of the spectrum. Earlier I said offense wins championships, but let's not undermine the need for defense. In the beginner section we discussed the skill of both attacking and defending. The "What can't I guard against question?" focuses on the defensive aspects of a game.

This is the question I think most people forget to ask themselves and focus on. It is important to determine what threat(s) you possess, but it is equally important to be aware of what threat(s) your opponent possesses and how they could lead to your downfall. Note, this doesn't mean you can always stop your opponent's threat but being aware of it can allow you to formulate a game plan that will minimize the casualties. The correct way to go about defending isn't as simplistic as the correct way to attack, however there are a few scenarios that I found necessary to point out. You will likely run into some variation of one of these when you battle:

Scenario 1:

- **"Do I have a Pokémon that if fainted will allow my opponent to sweep me?"**

Scenario 2:

- **"Do I have a Pokémon that if weakened, will allow my opponent to sweep me?"**

Scenario 1

- **"Do I have a Pokémon that if removed will allow my opponent to sweep me?"**

At team preview you notice that your opponent possesses a Volcarona, Garchomp, and Tapu Koko. You have a team with a Greninja, Scizor, and Rhyperior. Greninja has a Choice Scarf and knows the move Rock Slide, Gunk Shot, U-Turn, and Ice Beam. Volcarona has Life Orb and knows the moves Quiver Dance, Flamethrower, Bug Buzz, and Roost.

Looking at the team preview you ask the question, "What can't I guard against?". In a situation like this, Volcarona is lethal. It can OHKO every Pokémon on your team. Now you're asking, "Do I have a Pokémon that if removed will allow my opponent to sweep me?". If you were to allow your Greninja to be KO'd by any of his other Pokémon, then you would automatically lose to Volcarona after a Quiver Dance.

    I kept the number of Pokémon on each team at three to lesson any chance of confusion. The point is that Greninja needs to stay alive to keep that Volcorona at bay. Asking that question brought awareness to the fact that Volcarona is dangerous.

Scenario 2:

- **"Do I have a *Pokémon* that if weakened, will allow my opponent to sweep me?"**

At team preview you notice that your opponent possesses a Volcarona, Garchomp, and Tapu Koko. You have a team with a Slowbro, Scizor, and Salamence. Salamence has Lum Berry and knows the moves Rock Slide, Dragon Dance, Dragon Claw, and Roost. Volcarona has Life Orb and knows the moves Quiver Dance, Flamethrower, Bug Buzz, and Roost.

Looking at the team preview you ask the question, "What can't I guard against?". In a situation like this, Volcarona is lethal. It can KO two Pokémon on the team. Ask the question, "Do I have a Pokémon that if weakened will allow my opponent to sweep me?". Then, you'll realize that Salamence is that Pokémon. When at full health, Salamence can stop Volcarona and KO it with Rock Slide, however if Salamence is allowed to get to 50% or lower, Volcarona will be able to KO it after one Quiver Dance. Therefore, it is of the utmost importance to keep Salamence healthy in order to prevent the Volcarona from defeating your team.

Asking these questions are focused on the awareness pillar. Each question you ask draws out unconscious knowledge to conscious awareness. It is then that you can use your skill to achieve whatever outcome you desire. As I mentioned in the beginning, the two questions focus on the offensive capabilities, but you aren't limited to only those questions. You can also ask questions that focus on the defensive capabilities. One of which is: "What guards well against my opponent". This shifts your awareness away from your offensive prowess. Here's a scenario:

"Do I have Pokémon that guard against a large portion of his team?"

At team preview you notice that your opponent possesses a Volcarona, Keldeo, and Forretress. You have a team with a Mantine, Scizor, and Donphan. The opponent's Pokémon only have moves of their same type.

Looking at the team preview you ask the question, "What guards well against my opponent". In a situation like this, Mantine is near impossible to KO.

Nothing on the opponent's team can deal much damage. Mantine now holds a position that cannot be attacked. This is known as being an 'insurmountable wall'. Being an insurmountable wall means you can, by means of defensive tactics, put a halt to your opponent's threats. In other words, you have Pokémon that can check or counter your opponent's Pokémon.

A 'check' is a Pokémon that can handle a particular Pokémon, most of the time, without much issue. A 'counter' is a Pokémon that can always handle a particular Pokémon no matter the circumstance.

To employ this relies on possessing a strong defense. An example of this would be a person who, during a fist fight, blocks and absorbs the opponent's punches. Knowing they can take the hits; they patiently wait for the opponent to grow tired. This strategy relies on patience. When the opponent begins to wane, they deliver a few blows that deal a lot of damage. In the end, they are victorious. This is not necessarily due to possessing high power, though that can also be a reason, but more so because the opponent is weakened. Whether they themselves possess a lot of punching power is not what is important. Teams that focus on using this as their primary method of winning are known as 'stall' teams.

Chapter 5

Upper Intermediate

How to Practice Team Preview

After each battle, regardless of a loss or win, save the replay. After saving the replay,

pause at the team preview. Ensure the teams are positioned in the same way they are during

the actual battle. You have just played this battle, so you will likely remember it vividly.

This is where you focus on both teams intensively. The goal is to formulate a game plan, but not just any game plan; a game plan that gives you the highest likelihood of defeating your opponent while, simultaneously, protecting yourself against defeat. This does not mean you can't lose a Pokémon; it simply means in your game plan the opponent loses all six first. It's best to focus on how you intend to win first, then you focus on how to not lose to the opponent.

You can allow the battle to play after you've formulated a game plan to see where you could've applied it, but it is more important to focus on the team preview aspect. As I said before the team preview and the actual battle are not independent of each other, so many times they will bleed into each other. I will discuss how to practice improving your playing ability in subsequent chapters.

These will be known as your training sessions and make no mistake, they will be difficult. You will push your mental faculties to their absolute limits, and that's the best part. It is here that you grow. It may be stressful at times; it's a lot of information to process. But fret not! You're working at your own pace. Mastering this requires work and it will take time, so please be patient. Do not compare yourself to others. It would not surprise me if it takes you fifteen minutes or more to formulate a proper game plan, especially in the preliminary stages. You will need to invest time and effort on a consistent basis. Do that and you will improve; it's a simple formula.

During your practice sessions, there will be times where you will want to just click "Find Battle" without going through the reviewing process; this happens to me all the time, however, realize the decision to do so will only be to your detriment. The more effort you exert the sharper you will become. To take short cuts is to dull the blade. The ability to focus and stay consistent will be what separates players. At the end of the day, if you are not where you want to be you have only yourself to blame.

I would like to point out that this does not mean you have to be in a perpetual state of

practice. You don't need to do this every time you play *Pokémon*; sometimes you may want

to just play casually. Having fun is fine. Just ensure you separate the time you're playing

casually from the time you are practicing. Practice requires focus.

I am not inventing the wheel here. This applies in most areas in life. Professional athletes, for the greater good, endure training sessions where it's hard, monotonous, and

sometimes painful. They do this to hone their craft. This is no different. This is a skill.

During your more laid-back sessions, I would be wary of doing anything that goes

counter to what you do in training. So, if you completely disregard team preview with little to no thought for thirty games of casual play, while only focusing on it for seven games of practice, you will likely dilute the effects of the training session and experience slower growth.

Everything matters. This may seem intense and a lot more work and effort than you originally anticipated, but that is what it is going to take. There is a reason I started this book by describing the mind of a competitor. This isn't for everyone.

Leads (Intermediate)

"The onset of troops is like the rush of a torrent which will even roll stones along in its course." – Sun Tzu

The Pokémon you lead with can have a massive impact on the outcome of the game. At this point you should have determined what your plan of action is going to be, so now you must determine how you will commence that plan. The impact of the lead can impact a game far beyond the turn at hand. As such, it should not be taken lightly.

Choosing the incorrect lead could immediately propel you into a state of reaction on the first turn - this is not what you want. If possible, you want to always proactively enforce your will; you never want to be in reaction to your opponent. That isn't to say that you can't win if you must react, however you want to avoid this state as much as possible. Having proactive control means your game plan is in motion with the passing of each turn. If each turn is focused on stopping your opponent's game plan, then you are in a state of reaction. Whoever has proactive control of the game has the upper hand. You may not always be on the offensive but, at the end of each turn, your focus should be on how you can reverse this and conquer your opponent.

The reason people tend to disregard the lead is due to a thought process of, "I'll just switch to my check". This is entering the battle from a defensive standpoint. This is, from the onset, placing your opponent in a position of power. Pokémon battles are a battle of will. Both players want a certain outcome, but only one can get it. This does not mean you will always have an advantage on the lead, but you should want to.

You should always want to have the upper hand. This is a subtle idea because you may be thinking, "Who doesn't want the upper hand?". What I'd say to that is observe your actions. Players may sometimes get caught in the reactional cycle and focus all their thinking on how to survive rather than thrive. It then becomes a question of, "How can I protect myself?" rather than "How can I destroy my opponent?". It's important to know the answers to both questions but ultimately, you're aiming to defeat your opponent; whichever you focus on more will drive how you operate. A player using an offensive team while having the, "How can I protect myself?" mindset has maimed himself at the onset.

To truly determine the impact of different leads, one would have to reanalyze the same battle repeatedly while leading with a different Pokémon. We would then theorize about how the opponent would have reacted to that lead and so on. This is a lot of work. Obviously, no one does this which is why the importance of the lead is often overlooked.

This isn't to say the lead is the end all be all, but I wouldn't take it for granted. You must consider the long-term effects of your actions. In battle, information is key. If you are at a lead disadvantage and must switch, you involuntarily give your opponent information that you could have otherwise withheld.

Leads are especially important in situations where your opponent has something you can't guard against. If there is a Pokémon that gives you a hard time, whenever it enters the field, give it very few opportunities to be put into play. It would be incredibly foolish to lead with a Pokémon that has a disadvantage against a Pokémon you are unable to guard against; that would put you down one Pokémon on the first turn. The lead is also there for your own protection. The better your lead, the less you bleed.

How Select a Lead

Now that you've been provided with the context of why the lead is so critical, let's get into how to choose your lead. After determining your game plan, you want to bring to conscious awareness two things: Firstly, "What Pokémon does the opponent possess that you guard very poorly against?" Secondly, "What Pokémon do you possess that your opponent guards poorly against?". It's imperative to know these. Asking these activates the awareness pillar and helps provide some context as you enter battle.

Earlier I mentioned not going into battle with a reactive mindset; this is still the case. The reason you want to think about the opponent's threats first is because you never want to lead with a Pokémon that loses immediately to your opponent's biggest threat because that leaves you open from the onset of battle. Open here means the opponent has the potential to deal a significant amount of damage without you getting anything in return; your opponent can sap a lot of value from you. So, in this instance, select a Pokémon that prevents the most threatening Pokémon on the opponent's team from doing too much damage. Leading is about protection first and foremost and as the battle goes on you will still be focused on executing your game plan.

In the case of the second question, it is also important to be aware of the firepower you possess. If it is the case that you have several answers to the opponent's threats and have a Pokémon that is very hard for the opponent to guard against, it is permissible to select that as a lead even if that Pokémon doesn't provide protection. The reason this is ok is because that Pokémon's teammates can bear the burden of a poor lead match up. Only in this case should one lead in a non-protection manner.

These are general rules for selecting a lead. This is not an exhaustive list, however if you only abided by these two rules, then you'd still be able to excel to the highest level of play. I do not recommend trying to predict your opponent's lead without consideration for the greater implications it. Lead in a way that covers most, or all the openings your opponent could have.

Automatic Information

It may seem like you'll need to learn a ton of information in order to get great at this, and while that is true, there is hope. As you continually play, your knowledge bank will begin to expand. Your knowledge bank in this case is your memory. You will begin to expect certain things to happen without much thought because you've experienced those situations so many times before. When information is quickly processed without much conscious effort, we refer to this as 'automatic information'. This is important because you would be overloading your brain with information otherwise.

Your aim should be to automatize as much information as possible. This includes all metagame knowledge, what EV spreads Pokémon tend to use, how much they take from getting hit by certain moves, what moves the opposing Pokémon tend to use, the list goes on and on. Ideally, you want to have as much knowledge about the Pokémon within your metagame as possible so never stop learning! This is achieved by playing. This is why I stress playing so much because there is no shortcut for this experience. More play means more is added to your knowledge bank.

Your knowledge bank is only one piece to the puzzle of success. There is also the part of your brain that handles the processing of current and future events. We'll refer to it as your 'processor' and refer to the amount of room your brain has to process as 'mental ram'. The processor determines how many things can you focus on in a battle at the same time. The more efficient your processor, the more thoughts you can manage. This is different amongst players.

Mental ram on the other hand is similar across the board. Most people have the same amount of mental ram. Note that this is not to be confused with your knowledge bank. Your knowledge bank is your memory whereas mental ram is your finite capacity of focus. An example would be if I gave two people a task to wash cars. Each person receives one bucket of soapy water. Person number one manages to wash one car before he ran out of water. Person number two manages to wash three cars before he ran out of water. Both people washed the cars equally clean, however person number two is more efficient. In this example Each person is the processor, the bucket of water is the mental ram, and the cars are problems they aim to

What you'll come to learn about this game is that it's not only important to have knowledge, skill, and awareness, but also how quickly you can process and put into action these things. The speed of your processor is labeled as your 'processing power'. This is not to be confused with 'processing efficiency' which focuses how many different things you can focus on at once. Two players may be the same in each category, however, one is able to process information more quickly. Being able to process the information quickly gives you time to consider other things. If player one takes thirty seconds to process what player two can do in ten, then player two may be able to be three steps ahead in a way of looking at it.

"But how do I improve my processor, Jam?" Great question! Somebody wants to learn! You will improve your processor by the cycling of this process. You likely have already gone through these steps without realizing it, so it won't be anything overly complicated.

First, we start with the most foundational pillar - knowledge. You must increase your knowledge bank to its utmost; learn as much as you can about the metagame of your interest. You can do this by playing as many games as you can in that metagame, watching other people play, and/or reading up on it. Nothing new or special. It's always the same process when it comes to increasing the knowledge pillar.

Second, store solutions in your knowledge bank. This focuses on the skill pillar. When you encounter new situations, it can sometimes be the case that you get blindsided and/or defeated because you lacked either the knowledge, skill, or the awareness. After suffering that defeat, you will gain knowledge and awareness of that situation, but you may not have the skill to prevent it from happening again. This is one of the main reasons people have very little foresight. Most of their mental ram is concerned with trying to figure out the current turn. Until possible solutions for a problem are transferred to automatic information, they will always consume the most mental ram.

This does not always have to be the case, however; if you make the effort to transfer solutions, then that frees up more space to focus on other things beyond just the current moment. In order words, memorize what skills or strategy you'll need to deploy in order to solve the problem. This can be achieved by simply reviewing your battle after it is done and asking yourself, "What could I have done instead?" Simple. As a caveat, there will exist situations where there is nothing you could've been done to prevent an outcome; at that point it is an issue in how the team was constructed more so than finding the right solution. The person with the gun always wins in a fist fight.

The third step is to continually ask questions. You may follow the previous two steps to a T but in order to strengthen your foresight, you will need to constantly remain aware of where you are in relation to your game plan. There is no point in having a road map if you don't reference it.

You may be thinking that if you have all automatic information you won't need as much awareness, but that is far from the truth. You can never have too much awareness just like you can't have too much physical health. The more aware you are, the greater your advantage.

Knowledge and skill, at least partly, are under the dominion of your knowledge bank. Your level of awareness is the function of your processor. The information in your knowledge bank is static and doesn't change – though it can be added on to. For example, Toxapex's typing (poison and water) will never change, neither will it being weak to psychic, ground, and electric type moves. With your processor, information is constantly changing and being re-evaluated, hence emphasis on the importance of having peak awareness. As an example, Toxapex in my previous game may have been easier to defeat using my electric type moves, however in this game that is not the case because my opponent has different Pokémon paired with Toxapex. In this case, it may be easier to defeat it with my psychic type moves or my ground type moves. Having the ability to make these decisions is a byproduct of all the pillars in conjunction is your processor.

Double Switching (Intermediate)

"To secure ourselves against defeat lies in our own hands, but the opportunity of defeating the enemy is provided by the enemy himself." – Sun Tzu

Much like most of this chapter, we're going to take something you learned in the beginning chapter to the next level. You learned the concept of switching as a means of defending yourself in the beginning chapter, but that's not the only way to use switching. It can also be an offensive asset.

'Double switching' is the act of switching a Pokémon in just to switch it out without clicking a move. You may ask, why switch a Pokémon in just to switch it out? Good question. Basically, it's about gaining the upper hand. You may switch a Pokémon in on an opposing Pokémon's attack. But afterwards you realize that he will do the same to you, so instead of allowing switch in his counter or check as you attack, you switch out that Pokémon into another that beats the Pokémon he was going to switch into to beat yours! This prevents you from losing momentum. This is where the prediction aspect can get fun. It's all about having the upper hand!

This is just another level to the skill of switching. Another method to use to give yourself the edge over an opponent. The ability to do with will come after quite a bit of experience because you will need to know beforehand what the opponent will switch in to before you decide to double switch. You must be careful with this skill, however. When you double switch you don't attack that turn, so if the opponent does not switch into the Pokémon you were expecting, but instead stays in and attacks, you may find yourself in a bad situation.

So, when is the appropriate time to double switch? It ultimately comes down to your game plan. If in order to execute your game plan you need to have certain Pokémon on your team to be on the field against certain Pokémon of the opponent's then utilize this skill to its utmost, however if you do not need to double switch in order to carry out your game plan, then refrain from using it. It's a double-edged sword. Try not to get cut.

How to Improve Your Battling

Similarly, to how mastering the team preview requires practice in order to sharpen, improvement in battle will require the same. Buffering out the chinks in your battle execution will require the same tools I mentioned for practicing team preview. You will need to use Pokémon Showdown's replay function.

Unlike the team preview practice sessions, where your focus on what you could possibly do, the battle practice session will involve you knowing what already happened. You will be replaying each turn and ask the questions "did this aid my me in moving forward with my game plan?" and "did this also not leave me open to my opponent's game plan?" The dance, remember? You can also include after thoughts of the risk vs reward of certain plays you made, if you like, but that matters most during actual battle.

Since you already know your game plan, you know the outcome you'd like to achieve. It could be keeping a particular Pokémon healthy, or weakening a particular Pokémon so you can sweep with another. Whatever the case may be, your goal before the strike phase, is to prepare it.

While reviewing your plays, especially in games where you lost, think about what your game plan was. You lost that game likely due to not guarding yourself well enough against your opponent's game plan, or not striking when you had the opportunity. This is not true in every case, but it is a good foundational thought process to have.

Pause and think about the options you had that turn. Should you have switched? Did setting up entry hazards really help with your end goal? Was that play worth the risk? These are just a few questions among many that you may want to consider. After doing this for a while, you'll start being able to do it in battle more quickly, which in turn, will not only increase your wins, but also the ease to which you win. You will rarely make mistakes because you know your destination and how to get there.

There are times where there is genuinely nothing you could have done to prevail, but these are very few. Either way, you never want to entertain such thoughts; they simply provide an excuse and don't do much to foster growth. In all situations you must seek a way to win. Sometimes that may be relying on your opponent to make a mistake. That's perfectly fine. Whatever the case, a winner never enters battle believing he has already lost.

Advanced

(Working on Being More Precise)

Chapter 6

Lower Advanced

The Value Dynamic

"Hence a wise general makes a point of foraging on the enemy. One cartload of the enemy's provisions is equivalent to twenty of one's own, and likewise a single picul of his provender is equivalent to twenty from one's own store" – *Sun Tzu*

According to the dictionary, 'value' is the importance, worth, or usefulness of something. In *Pokémon* it is the same. "Value? What are you talking about Jam?". Slow down star student, I'm about to tell you! Value is the currency that drives your decisions.

What you will come to learn is, in battle, there are good and bad decisions. This then begs the question, "How can you tell?" This is where understanding the value dynamic comes into play.

This is a very similar idea to purpose, but it is slightly different. The value dynamic is more of an overarching idea. Upon entering battle, both players possess a finite amount of value. With each turn that goes by in battle, players are often either losing value or gaining value. Players are either getting closer to their end goal or falling further away from it.". Value is a measurement for how much progress you're making.

The value of something can vary with each situation. How much value something possesses is determined, primarily, by how you intend to win. If a particular Pokémon, item, etc. is unnecessary with regards to the win condition, then in that context it possesses little to no value. As stated before, a thing of value will have a definitive purpose.

Two things could possess equal objective value but unequal subjective value. Objective value refers to what it innately possesses. Example: Ferrothorn is a grass and steel type. This is a fact. Ferrothorn x4 resists grass. That's a fact. Most would agree that Ferrothorn has good stats and is a good Pokémon; it has high objective value. However, if Ferrothorn, being x4 times weak to fire, is used against a team of six fire types, then despite being a good Pokémon objectively it will have very low value in this situation. If Ferrothorn were to face a team of pure water types, then its subjective value would be very high. This is an important consideration.

Whenever you gain value your opponent loses value. The person who wins is the person who takes all the value from the other person. This is why I referred to it as a dynamic. There is generally always going to be a constant exchange of value throughout a game. That's ok, if you win the game. The long term is really what should drive your immediate plays and your value exchanges. It may be beneficial to sacrifice some value in the short term because in the long run you will regain a substantial amount.

Team Preview (Categorizing)

"If you know the enemy and you know yourself, you need not fear the results of a hundred battles." – Sun Tzu

In the intermediate section I really hammered the importance of a game plan; in this section we will be focusing on categorizing battles so that you can gain context for your game plan from the onset. This tactic allows you to operate at a higher level of awareness immediately which will give you the edge. At the advanced level of play, most of your opponents will be competent, so you'll need a little more than knowledge and skill to separate yourself. It's all about awareness and foresight here. Skill and knowledge won't fluctuate too much.

There are three categories I've come up with for the type of game plans: 'Set Up and Sweep', 'Blow for Blow', and 'Walking a Tight Rope'. I will go into detail as to what each entail and it won't be difficult to see why this would be useful.

Set Up and Sweep

Most people generally go into a game with this battle perspective. The Set Up and Sweep refers to a situation where one or more of your Pokémon has the potential to defeat at least four members on the opponent's team. It may require that certain conditions be met first or it may not. Either way, simply being aware of this will be huge.

Set Up and Sweep immediately allows you to focus on your strengths and your opponent's weaknesses. Due to its simplicity, this is a reason most people choose to use it; however, I'd only advise this when you have an advantage after evaluating the teams. An advantage in this case means you have Pokémon that are incredibly threatening and defeat the opponent's six Pokémon before they have a chance to retaliate. This is the ideal situation; generally, in this position, if you formulate a solid game plan and make no mistakes you will prevail.

This type of battle, as the name suggests is centered around Pokémon that have the potential to 'boost'. In this case, boost doesn't only refer to moves that boost your stats but also refers to abilities and field conditions. In *Pokémon* there are moves that boost stats which can allow a Pokémon's threat level to increase significantly. There are also abilities that can boost a Pokémon's stats under certain circumstances such as Moxie, Beast Boost, or Contrary just to name a few. Last but not least, are field conditions. With field conditions a Pokémon can sweep if, and only if, the correct forces are in place. These can be things such as

Weather conditions, Terrain boosts, Trick Room, and even Entry Hazards. This is the most expansive because it can change from the battle to battle. These forces are independent of the Pokémon itself, but aids in paving the way for it to perform.

Blow for Blow

The second type is what I call Blow for Blow. This occurs when two teams are relatively even. This can be deduced after performing the assessment and realizing that there are no glaring weaknesses in either of the teams. At this point, it becomes a battle of patience and strategy. This is the purest form of battle because at this point, assuming no hax, the players will be having a full bout of wits. It is in this type of battle that the principles you've learned will be most important. If both players are competent then these will tend to be longer battles

Walking a Tight Rope

The last, but certainly not least, of the three I've termed Walking a Tight Rope. This type of game refers to one in which you have a very poor match up, so you'll have to play with a higher degree of risk in order to prevail. This a "your back is against the wall" kind of game. You realize that your opponent has several ways to defeat you, so rather than playing their game at their pace you will be very aggressive in your style of execution. This is representative of not allowing any of the opponent's Pokémon that will lose you a lot of the value to enter the field without being punished. In these kinds of games, it is not always possible to win but trying and failing is far better than giving up at the onset.

Recognizing and executing on each category will require all three pillars. The knowledge to know what the Pokémon on the opposing team do, the skill to assess the team preview, which then heightens your awareness as a result.

Awareness is really what you'll be accessing when you categorize a battle. Now that you know the type of battle you are in; you can now create a game plan with a lot more precision. These categories are guides to aid in accessing a deeper level of awareness. The order of actions at team preview can now be seen as such: assessment, categorization, then game plan.

Gathering Information

"By discovering the enemy's dispositions and remaining invisible ourselves, we can keep our forces concentrated, while the enemy's must be divided" – Sun Tzu

While assessing team preview, you will be speculating what your opponent's Pokémon are tailored to do because it is impossible to know, with absolute certainty, the items, moves, abilities, and EV spreads. For this very reason, it is imperative that you go into battle cautiously in the beginning to avoid being blindsided by something you did not account for. What you'll be doing to the early portions of the game is, particularly in a Blow for Blow, engaging in a process known as 'information gathering'. The game plan you have decided to go with is only a theory until you've gathered the necessary information to determine if it is executable. You may discover during your excursion that a Pokémon possess something that impedes or completely shuts down your original win condition. It is not wise to fully commit to a game plan without first knowing some information about the opponent's Pokémon. There are instances where you can do so without much consequence, but as a rule of thumb, always try to gather information. This is less true in the case of a Walking a Tight Rope type of battle where you may not have the luxury of gathering information.

This skill requires patience. Often, players will early in battle, attempt to finish their opponent without gathering enough information, only to lose their win condition. You may possess a set up sweeper that you could attempt to win with within the first five turns of battle, but the opponent has a potential counter measure that could thwart your plans. You could choose to risk it; you could try and get revenge-killed, or you could play for an extra twenty or so turns to gather information and then decide whether it's safe to do so. There are times where the opponent does have an unexpected counter measure, so you'll need to adapt and formulate a new win condition.

Sometimes at team preview, you may try guessing what the opponent's sets will likely be; this is fine, but I recommend never taking these guesses as fact. Until you see it, it's theory. It may make sense for it to be that, but until your assumption is proven true, always air on the side of caution.

It must be noted that while the information gathering process is taking place, you are still focused on your win condition. Never disregard that. You might not know if it's possible but keep it in mind. You're at an advanced level now, so the skills introduced here will be more about heightening your awareness because that's what will ascend you to the Mastery level.

Positioning

"Therefore, the clever combatant imposes his will on the enemy, but does not allow the enemy's will to be imposed on him." - Sun Tzu

Positioning is a skill that has offensive and defensive utility. It is the act of performing an action that limits the range of options an opponent has. It is a very subtle way of forcing your will onto an opponent. Think of it as an 'if, then' manner. If I do this, then my opponent must do that. Performing this correctly requires one to have awareness of whatever outcome they are trying to achieve and prevent, hence the offensive and defensive duality to this skill.

Following the 'if, then' line of thought, we're going to discuss how this can be utilized defensively. Positioning should be thought of as an indirect way of controlling certain outcomes. Let's say there is a situation where your opponent possesses a Pokémon, that if sent in, places you at risk of losing a significant amount of value. You would need to ensure that you deploy a Pokémon that can offensively threaten the opponent's own Pokémon. This is an offensive means of guarding against threats. We will call this 'Defensive – Offensive' positioning because despite the fact that though you are using your Pokémon to be threatening, you are doing so as a means of protection ultimately. By doing this, you limit what the opponent can send in, and thus indirectly controlling their actions. It would be akin to if you deterred an enemy with the fact that you have a gun that can kill them before they get to harm you. They may want to attack you, but refrain because they are fearful of being shot.

As you very well know, there are also defensive ways to position yourself for protection. This is achieved by simply switching in a Pokémon that can switch to the opponent's attack and lose little to no value. We will call this 'pure defensive' positioning. Instead of using your offensive prowess to dissuade the opponent, you use your defensive prowess. This follows the same 'if, then' principles. "If my opponent chooses to attack with this Pokémon, then I'll use *this* Pokémon to guard against it", thus controlling the amount of value the opponent can receive. This is akin to protecting yourself with a shield that an opponent can't break.

Positioning can also be utilized outside of the realm of defense. It can also be used to coerce your opponent into doing something they did not want to. If you have a particular outcome you want to achieve that your opponent is desperately trying to avoid, then you use positioning to give him no other choice. If the opponent doesn't perform the action you want them to, then they risk losing a massive amount of value. This creates an ultimatum.

In order to do this, you will need to be well-versed with the metagame and have a proper game plan set up. By having a game plan, you know what conditions need to be met for you to be victorious. In order for these conditions to be met you may need to coerce your opponent into performing certain actions by placing out baits that cannot be avoided without great risk. Since the opponent chose not to perform said action, they lost a considerable amount of value, which will result in them losing no matter what they do. Always remember to reference the if, then!

Chapter 7

Upper Advanced

Deception

"Hence, when able to attack, we must seem unable; when using our forces, we must seem inactive; when we are near, we must make the enemy believe we are far away; when far away, we must make him believe we are near." – Sun Tzu

Deception is a tactic in where you try to get your opponent to believe some piece of information is true, when in all reality it is false. It is purposefully withholding information until your opponent has grown comfortable. The point of having them believe this is to have them lower their guard so you can achieve a particular outcome. It's a tool aimed at having the opponent lower their awareness. When this happens, and your opponent has gained confidence, you strike him down with an unsuspected blow. Below is an example of its application.

You have a team of three Pokémon: Keldeo, Heatran, Zapdos Your opponent has a team of Salamence, Tentacruel, and Ferrothorn. Keldeo has the item Choice Scarf. Heatran has the item Life Orb. Zapdos has the item Leftovers. Keldeo knows the moves Surf, Secret Sword, and Icy Wind. Heatran knows the moves Flamethrower and Earth Power. Zapdos knows the move Thunderbolt. Salamence has the item Draconium Z. Tentacruel has the item Black Sludge. Magnezone has the item Leftovers. Salamence knows the moves Dragon Dance, Outrage, and Earthquake. Tentacruel knows the moves Surf and Rapid Spin. Magnezone knows the moves Volt Switch and Flash Cannon. It must be noted that Keldeo and Salamence are the important Pokémon in this scenario. The other members are here as fillers, as are their moves.

Now, here's the situation. Salamence can kill every Pokémon on your team if it gets a Dragon Dance up. It has the Moxie ability. Heatran's Flamethrower requires four hits to KO. Zapdos is faster than Salamence and its Thunderbolt can KO in two hits, however, if Salamence gets up a Dragon Dance, Zapdos will be OHKO. If the opponent loses his Salamence, then his remaining two will have a tough time with Zapdos and Heatran. Keldeo, generally cannot do much damage to Salamence, but sometimes carry the Icy Wind. Icy wind is an OHKO on Salamence. If the Keldeo is not carrying Icy Wind, it will be a simple victory. With that information in mind, let's commence the game.

You lead Keldeo. Your opponent leads Salamence. Turn one: your opponent switches Salamence out into Tentacruel. You switch your Keldeo out into Zapdos. Turn two: the opponent switches Tentacreul out into Magnezone as Zapdos goes for Thunderbolt. Turn three: Zapdos switches out into Heatran. Magnezone uses Volt Switch. Your opponent sends out Salamence. Turn four: You switch Heatran out into Keldeo. Salamence goes for Dragon Dance. Turn five: Keldeo uses Icy Wind, Salamence Faints. Your opponent then forfeits.

What happened here? This, my friends, was an extremely simplified simulation of deception in action. The opponent switched out Salamence into Tentacruel attempting to do some 'information gathering'. You instead switched into Zapdos. Now, your opponent is under the impression that Keldeo lacks the Icy Wind. So, when he got the opportunity to Dragon Dance, he did so in confidence. His guard was down. At this point, you unveil the Icy Wind OHKOing his Salamence. He can no longer win the game.

Be wary of deception, while being deceitful. Information gathering is not a one-way street.

Risk vs. Reward

"The general who thoroughly understands the advantages that accompany variation of tactics knows how to handle his troops. The general who does not understand these, may be well acquainted with the configuration of the country, yet he will not be able to turn his knowledge to practical account." - Sun Tzu

Throughout this book, I've emphasized the importance of the big picture. Framework is very important, but let's not make the mistake of undervaluing the importance of each individual turn. At the beginning of each turn, you will need to assess the risk of making a move versus the reward of making a move. A risk is what you may lose, while a reward is what you may gain.

Often, players do not properly consider 'risk vs. reward'. After playing a metagame for long enough, players tend to develop auto-pilot responses to certain situations. This requires very little thought and makes for fast-paced playing. Doing this actually decreases your awareness levels. Thought is the very thing you need most. With every turn, building up to whatever your game plan is, you want to be constantly assessing risk vs. reward. Constantly. The more you do it, the less time and mental energy it will require. Initially, this will prove difficult. It all comes back to practice. Practice is always the answer. It's a pain, but no true skill comes without effort.

Categories of Risk vs. Reward

There are four different situations you will find yourself in when contemplating risk vs. reward: high risk, high reward; low risk, low reward; high risk, low reward; low risk, high reward.

A **<u>high risk, high reward situation</u>** refers to a turn where you are at risk of losing a lot of value, while your opponent is at risk of losing a lot of value.

A **<u>low risk, low reward situation</u>** refers to a situation where not much value is at stake, but you don't gain much either.

A **<u>high risk, low reward situation</u>** refers to a situation where you have a lot of value to lose, while gaining very little back.

A **<u>low risk, high reward situation</u>** refers to a situation where you risk very little value but could gain a tremendous amount in return.

The ability to properly assess this may be the great divide between players higher on the totem pole. Many players may assess this a few times during battle, but the ability to constantly take it into consideration is not an easy task. This does not only apply to how you can inflict damage, but also to how much your risk leaving yourself open to counter attacks.

High Risk, High Reward

You have a Tapu Lele and a Scizor. Your opponent has a Blissey and a Heatran. Your Tapu Lele has the moves Psyshock and Hidden Power Ground. Your Scizor knows Bullet Punch and U-Turn. Your opponent's Heatran knows Flash Cannon and Flamethrower. Your opponent's Blissey knows Flamethrower and Soft-Boiled. Flash Cannon is an OHKO on Tapu Lele. Hidden Power Ground is an OHKO on Heatran. Psyshock is an OHKO on Blissey. Flamethrower is an OHKO on Scizor from both Blissey and Heatran. Tapu Lele has the item Choice Specs. Heatran has the item Leftovers. Blissey has the Item Leftovers. Scizor has the item Leftovers.

Turn one: you lead Tapu Lele while your opponent leads Heatran. It's time for your risk vs. reward assessment.

Scenario 1:

- If you go for Hidden Power Ground as your opponent switches to Blissey. Blissey will defeat Tape Lele, while Tapu Lele's Hidden Power Ground does very little damage. Blissey then either beats Tapu Lele with Flamethrower or KOs Scizor as you try to switch out. Thus, your opponent wins.

Scenario 2:

- If you go for Psyshock with Tapu Lele as your opponent switches to Blissey, you will OHKO it, leaving only Heatran. You then allow your Scizor to be KO'd. Afterwards, you go back to

Tapu Lele and KO Heatran with Hidden Power Ground. Thus, your win.

Scenario 3:

- If you go for Psyshock as Tapu Lele as your opponent stays in with Heatran, you do roughly 40% as Tapu Lele gets OHKO'd by Flash Cannon. Heatran then proceeds to OHKO Scizor with Flamethrower. Thus, your opponent wins.

Scenario 4:

- If you go for Hidden Power Ground as Tapu Lele as your stays in with Heatran you OHKO. At this point you can allow Scizor to be

OHKO'd, switch Tape Lele back in and OHKO Blissey with Psyshock.

Low Risk, High Reward

You have a Gengar and a Greninja. Your opponent has a Chansey and a Latios. Your Gengar has the moves Shadow Ball, Sludge Wave, and Taunt. Your Greninja knows Surf and Dark Pulse. Your opponent's Chansey knows Seismic Toss and Soft-Boiled. Your opponent's Latios knows Draco Meteor and Psyshock. Draco Meteor is an OHKO on Gengar and Greninja. Shadow Ball is an OHKO on Latios. Chansey cannot harm Gengar. Greninja OHKOs Latios with Dark Pulse. Latios has the item Life Orb. Greninja has the item Choice Specs. Chansey has the Item Eviolite. Gengar has the item Life Orb.

Turn one: You lead Gengar while your opponent leads Chansey. It's time for your risk versus reward assessment.

For the low risk situation, I will not list the possible scenarios. This one is very straightforward. Seeing as Chansey is incapable of threatening the Gengar, Gengar can freely click the move Shadow Ball despite Chansey not being affected by it. If Chansey stays in, Gengar receives no punishment (low risk); if Chansey switches out to Latios while Gengar uses Shadow Ball, then Latios gets OHKO'd (high reward). You have very little to lose if you do not make the correct prediction.

I will point out that there were different possibilities to consider such as PP and Chansey potentially switching out on a turn Gengar uses Taunt, but the main point of the example is the illustrate a low risk, high reward scenario.

High Risk, High Reward

You have a Landorus and a Blacephalon. Your opponent has a Volcanion and Skarmory. Your Landorus has the moves Earthquake and Stealth Rock. Your Blacephalon knows Shadow Ball and Flamethrower. Your opponent's Volcanion knows Steam Eruption. Your opponent's Skarmory knows Roost and Iron Head. Flamethrower is an OHKO on Skarmory. Earthquake is an OHKO on Volcanion. Shadow Ball is a 2HKO on Skarmory and Volcanion. Steam Eruption is an OHKO on both Landorus and Blacephalon. Landorus has the item Earth Plate. Skarmory has the item Leftovers. Volcanion has the item Splash Plate. Blacephalon has the item Life Orb.

Turn one: You lead Landorus while your opponent leads Volcanion. You use Stealth Rock anticipating Volcanion to switch out fearing the OHKO, but your opponent instead uses Steam Eruption. Your Landorus is now gone. Blacephalon can no longer OHKO Volcanion, while Volcanion can OHKO Blacephelon. Your loss.

Using Stealth Rock (high risk) was not worth the damage Skarmory and Volcanion would receive upon switching in (low reward). This example is not perfect, but it does illustrate the idea well enough. Setting up Stealth Rock was not necessary in order to win.

Low Risk, Low Reward

You have a Chansey and a Mew. Your opponent has a Medicham and a Greninja. Your Chansey has the moves Seismic Toss and Soft-Boiled. Your Mew knows Soft-Boiled and Thunderbolt. Your opponent's Medicham knows High Jump Kick and Zen Headbutt. Your opponent's Greninja knows Dark Pulse and Surf. Dark Pulse is an OHKO on Mew. High Jump Kick is an OHKO on Chansey. Chansey has the item Eviolite. Greninja has the item Choice Specs. Medicham has the item Choice Scarf. Mew has the item Leftovers.

In this scenario I will not discuss the event of the first turn because ultimately it doesn't matter. If the lead is Mew vs. Greninja, then you can switch to Chansey (low risk) and wall Greninja (low reward). If the opponent anticipates your switch to Chansey and goes to Medicham, then you can always switch back to Mew (low risk) and wall the Medicham (low reward).

Strike

"What is essential in war is victory, not prolonged operations." - Sun Tzu

Much like deception, originally, I did not intend to dedicate much time to the idea of finishing your opponent. I felt it obvious enough, however I feel there are a few nuances I'd should to go over. "Strike while the iron is hot", a well-known saying; but how does it apply to *Pokémon*? Much like a heated piece of iron possesses a finite time span in which it can be molded, a Pokémon battle possesses a finite time span in which it can be won. During battle, a time will come where you can win the game if you 'strike'; the time to put the nail in the coffin. Hitherto this moment, you may be patiently waiting as you or your opponent create the necessary conditions for victory. When this happens, you must act. You must finish your opponent. The time for scouting and gathering information is over. To allow this moment to pass, is to throw victory to the wayside. This is not to say other opportunities cannot arise, but it would be akin to having to reheat the iron. Once the iron has gone cold, it is less pliable

    The question now arises, "How do I know when that time is?". The answer to this will depend on what your game plan is. There is no one answer. Only through constant playing and practice can your ability to recognize these moments sharpen.

Choke

"He wins his battles by making no mistakes. Making no mistakes is what establishes the certainty of victory, for it means conquering an enemy that is already defeated." - Sun Tzu

This is related to striking, but I decided to discuss it separately. The act of choking is a very common occurrence among players. Choking refers to providing your opponent with an opportunity to win, when you already had the battle won. Note that I said, "you provide". Choking is not your opponent making exceptional plays and creating opportunities, choking is defeating *yourself*. This stems from a person not striking while the iron is hot. It does not apply only to offensive tactics, however. A player may have a key

Pokémon that guards against the opponent's biggest threat, but unnecessarily allows it to be KO'd or weakened. This in turn creates an opening that was avoidable. This is gifting your opponent a second chance when there should've been none.

In order to avoid this, you will need to first stop and assess the value of each Pokémon you possess. This is a time for heightened awareness. Ask yourself, "How can my opponent get back in this game?" and "What can't the opponent guard against?". This then triggers awareness of what not to do, allowing you to figure out what to do. After realizing that, you can better navigate what needs to be done in order to properly finish off the opponent.

There is no one answer for how to prevent choking. The questions I provided were only two of the many that can be asked, however these for the most part will point you in the right direction with regards to your awareness.

Mastery

(Making No Mistakes)

Chapter 8

The Master

Congratulations! You're almost at the peak of the mountain! You've come a long way and I am genuinely proud of you. In the Mastery section there will be less emphasis on doing this or that, and more on the attributes that are necessary. At this point you should be well versed in all the skills and knowledge you need to be one of the best you may just need little tweaks in your mindset to put you in that next tier.

Patience

"The good fighters of old first put themselves beyond the possibility of defeat, and then waited for an opportunity of defeating the enemy. To secure ourselves against defeat lies in our own hands, but the opportunity of defeating the enemy is provided by the enemy himself." - Sun Tzu

Patience is one of the subtle attributes that separates the very good player from a master. Often, players perceive patience as being passive, this is far from the truth. What they are assuming when thinking of patience is where they are in their development as a player. Patience in *this* case means waiting for the victory that is already yours. This is where a lot of the earlier concepts become critical. If you have assessed the opponent's team, determined what category of battle it is, and created a game plan, then you now have a road map. Follow that map. As discussed in *The Art of War*, the opponent creates the opportunity for victory. You can encourage him to perform certain actions, but ultimately that's how it is. You must wait for the opportunity to strike.

Let's say you had to drive to a job interview. You need to be there in 30 minutes, so you put the destination in your GPS, and it provides a route that will allow you arrive in 25 minutes guaranteed. This means you will arrive at your destination on-time; you'll just have to stick to the route. You're ok with this and start your journey. Midway in your journey you see what you believe will be a shortcut. If you take this shortcut, it could get you there five minutes faster than the guaranteed route. Now you have a decision to make. Do you stick to the predetermined route that will get you the outcome you want guaranteed but may take longer? Or, do you take the short cut that has a chance of you getting the outcome you want faster? In this case, you decide to take the shortcut and end up running into a car accident which delays the trip by 15 minutes. So, instead of taking 25 minutes to get there, you will now take 35 minutes. You are now late and missed out on the job interview and opportunity. You lost. This analogy reflects the importance of patience in a battle.

There was a reason I equipped you with skills prior to this section. Most players defeat themselves by providing openings due to their impatience. A master of this will cycle through all the necessary skills for as long as necessary, deploy as many faints as necessary and gather as much information as possible before deciding when the appropriate time to strike will be. A master will take 30 turns if it means a guaranteed win than try to win in five turns if it's a 90% chance. The guaranteed win is always better.

Foresight (Extreme Awareness)

"It is said that if you <u>know</u> your <u>enemies</u> and know yourself, you will not be imperiled in a hundred battles; if you do not know your enemies but do know yourself, you will win one and lose one; if you do not know your enemies nor yourself, you will be imperiled in every single battle." - Sun Tzu

In earlier sections we discussed the idea of foresight. In this section I will be expounding on it a bit more because it is subtle yet crucial. Foresight at this level is beyond just knowing what the opponent will do; it is assessing all the possibilities of particular actions. It's seeing the game's potential ending before it even begins.

When you have practiced consistently to the point where you know the intricacies of that metagame like the back of your hand, your processing power and efficiency will exceed that of even advanced players. It will reach a level where it seems like you can see the future, and in a way you can. Now you require so little mental ram to focus on the current turn through constant repetition, that you gain the ability to see several turns ahead of the current one. This is a massive advantage because it everything changes that you've learned up to this point – in a good way. Your game plans are incredibly intricate and specific because of the vast amount of knowledge you've obtained, your interactions with the value dynamic are on a whole different level because you have a lot more context, and your deployment of your skills will be very precise because you know exactly what outcome you are trying to achieve. Attaining this level of awareness is something only a few ever achieve.

In order to get to this level, you will need to practice. You will need to follow the process I outlined in the earlier chapters and do not skip a step. Remember, your aim is to speed up your processing power to extreme levels and in order to do so you must train. Get so gelled with the metagame of your choosing to the point where almost no situation surprises you. It is just another day in the office as far as you're concerned. Over time, you will use a far less mental ram for things that may use up most mental ram of other players. This gives way to the birth of your extreme foresight.

Never Rest on Your Laurels

Man, what a ride. We're at the end. I figured it would be fitting to add this in the end because it's a pitfall I've seen players fall prey to and that I've fallen prey to several times throughout my journey and that is 'resting on your laurels'. I'm basically saying, if you're aiming to compete, never get too comfortable and think you've arrived. When you don't practice this and maintain the information you've learned in this book, it will start to wane. You will start to stagnate or get worse. This doesn't mean you can't win games anymore, but it does mean you're no longer among the elite. You're no longer a master. So, remember, always keep the machine oiled. If you don't use it, you'll lose it.

Thank You

Thank you for taking the time to read this book. This is my *Pokémon* legacy. I truly want to see competitive *Pokémon* be great again. I want to have an environment where everyone is competent, there are no excuses, and people are having a good time. For the last time, go forth and play.

Printed in Great Britain
by Amazon